Burning Down Disneyland

Also from Gunpowder Press:

The Tarnation of Faust: Poems by David Case

Mouth & Fruit: Poems by Chryss Yost

Shaping Water: Poems by Barry Spacks

Original Face: Poems by Jim Peterson

Instead of Sadness: Poems by Catherine Abbey Hodges

What Breathes Us: Santa Barbara Poets Laureate, 2005-2015
Edited by David Starkey

Shoreline Voices Projects:

Buzz: Poets Respond to SWARM
Edited by Nancy Gifford and Chryss Yost

Rare Feathers: Poems on Birds & Art
Edited by Nancy Gifford, Chryss Yost, and George Yatchisin

BURNING DOWN DISNEYLAND

POEMS

KURT OLSSON

GUNPOWDER PRESS • SANTA BARBARA
2017

Published by Gunpowder Press
David Starkey, Editor
PO Box 60035
Santa Barbara, CA 93160-0035

Cover image: *Nocturne in Black and Gold —The Falling Rocket,*
        James McNeill Whistler
Back cover photo: Rob Grossman
ISBN-13: 978-0-9916651-9-8

www.gunpowderpress.com

For Nadiya and Brianna

ACKNOWLEDGMENTS

Grateful acknowledgment is given to the following journals where versions of these poems have appeared or are forthcoming:

Alaska Quarterly Review: "Tocsin" and "To Guilt"

Antioch Review: "Lent"

Boulevard: "Ball" and "The Good for Nothing and Left for Dead"

FIELD: "Kilimanjaro" and "De Kooning's Shirt"

Folio: "City of the Infinite Lie"

Gettysburg Review: "Small Change," "Bait," "Johnny Quest," "True Genius," and "Some Stories"

Mid-American Review: "I Won't Need Billy Collins Anymore" and "The Stars Are Too Far to Need Faces"

The New Republic: "Nobody's Sonnet"

Passages North: "Just Once"

Poet Lore: "Trespasses," "Cleanly," and "Afterwards"

Poetry East: "How You Will Remember Me When I'm Dead and Buried"

River Styx: "The Way Things Work" and "Blackout Drinking"

Southern Review: "Life on a Smaller Planet"

The author would also like to thank the Vermont Studio Center where early versions of many of these poems first saw the light of day.

CONTENTS

Darkness is essential.

—*Steve Martin*

Life on a Smaller Planet

One day, you wake up, what the hell,
and unscrew your ears. You wrap them in cellophane
and keep them in the freezer,
just in case you get nostalgic. Such small
things, yet they weigh so much:
you feel strangely buoyant, as if you'd blasted
to another planet and gravity no longer
played such havoc. You miss a lot, sure.
You have to stare at people's mouths now,
marvel at the Gothic architecture of their teeth,
some upright and polished like
a military salute, others a Lichtenstein of bowling pins
and a word balloon screaming "Pow" or "Bam."
When someone takes your hand
to help you cross the street, you read the future
in the arid rasp of *au revoir* of her palm.
The benefits: you come to admire
the attitudes of folding chairs,
their Midwestern manner of never intruding,
even when left alone. Oddly,
lying in bed late is when
you miss the pair most, the weak static they picked up:
the lone insomniac car
daring the interstate, a dog far off
and its philosophic pronouncement of its dogness, the fall wind
tickling the night's small, golden change from the trees.

How Many Angels

And afterward where do they all go
spilling from the pin's head like wildflowers
dried and forgotten in an unread book?

And what happens to their music?
Does it stop or do the notes still jig and echo
like tin horns in the cities of the damned?

What comes of the slippers and the tambours,
pan flutes and lyres, all the instruments
of their useless dancing?

And what of the angel,
last numbered, one metaphysical foot lifted
for his first and forever final dance step?

Kilimanjaro

There's always a light at the end of the tunnel,
but I'm not in a tunnel, it's a train station,
and that isn't a light, it's my dog sneaking out
the screen door, but as I run to get closer,
it isn't my dog, it's something skittering about
like a bar napkin aflame with writing in a hand
I can't decipher, except I'm not running,
no matter how I pump my legs, my knees clogged
with thumb tacks and peanut butter,
I'm thumping along like a ninety-year-old,
my mind still blue heat like a GTO's muffler
but my body an anthill eroding on Kilimanjaro—
Kilimanjaro a word I long to spell out sing-song—
but now I'm at the tiller of a sailboat,
sobbing as I sizzle down a highway
lethal as an alley in a kung-fu movie,
I see bottom, every life-wrecking rock, every sunk
tree trunk, yet the keel slices neat as a straight razor,
I skate over faces crying up at me, veer onto
the shoulder sometimes, but it doesn't matter,
just as it didn't when in kindergarten I peed on stage,
I'm going to make it, nobody will notice,
then—wham!—it's just me in a room
with a silver stand, shimmering like a candelabra,
a single sheet jammed with notes in the bass clef,
but I never studied the bass clef,
I played clarinet, here it is melting in my fingers,
if I can still be said to have fingers,
and there's this clicking, maybe a tongue clucking,

maybe a hand flipping a light switch over
and over again, and every face I've ever loved
is watching, breathless for the solo I see now
I should've practiced every second of my life.

All God's Creatures

About the flies no one speaks:
the muzzy mass descending onto

Christ's face and hair, mouth and sex,
his delicious wounds.

Nor that the flies sipped oblivion
from his lips, his eyeballs,

then zithered away, warm in their insubstantial
share of him.

The dusk must have shimmered sweeter.
The unruly unknown

tugging them down to earth, for a time,
a trifle weaker.

Terra Incognita

Washington, D.C.

Man bends over desk,
holds up his hands,
palms to himself,
fanning out scarred pink.
Warming to the story now, sloughing
off the dust from the gov't job.
See these, he says, these
hands might make you think
I did harm to myself,
but they're from there,
air so moist you
so much as rub against metal
skin peels clean off. Says,
the Dinka that got religion's
the worst kind,
fellow that read the Bible
yesterday suddenly knows
more than all of us.
Says, got a son, a good boy,
twenty-five, can't get a job,
reads Shakespeare,
can quote Shakespeare,
but no mind for tests.
Says, I'd go back in a heartbeat:
walked every road (aren't many),
crossed every bridge (even fewer).
Says, there living's the issue,
you go, take nothing
but valium and a straitjacket.

Trespasses

The monks do not wish to be observed
the signpost said in five languages.

I entered, hushed,
a parking lot and a brick wall.

By the only door, a red telephone booth.
I imagined rain falling, each soul's brief

transparency.

Nobody's Sonnet

Nobody understands when I write in the dark.
When nobody writes in the dark I understand.

I write in the dark when nobody understands.
In the dark when I understand nobody writes.

I understand when nobody writes in the dark.
When I write in "nobody" the dark understands.

I understand when the dark in nobody writes.
Understand the dark in nobody when I write.

When in the dark I write nobody, understand?
I write: when in nobody, the dark understands.

When I write in dark the nobody understands.
When in nobody I understand the dark writes.

The dark nobody writes in—I understand when.
In the dark, write: when I understand nobody.

Nobody understands when I write in the dark.
Nobody understands when I write the dark in.

Small Change

I couldn't love him for the wart,
foreign imperfection wobbling like

a nipple on his cheek when he chewed
or laughed. He reminded me of a snowman,

one old, unschooled lump atop another.
Though mother said it rude, he let me

rifle through his trouser pockets as he stood there,
when pockets were meant for what

a worker needed in a day—penknife,
keys, ink-smeared rubber-band cinching a roll

of green, bus token, a stray roasted chestnut—
and the week's change he'd dig up

and drop into my pale, cupped palms,
coin by coin, like a catechism, until

they almost overflowed. I knew
rare dates and odd circulations,

just as I knew I'd uncover a treasure others
couldn't and he wondered at that, calling me

his brilliant boy, and I, despite the wart,
never managing to disbelieve him.

Lent

You decide
to give up forks.
It isn't much
of a concession.
You prefer spoons
better anyway.
More dependable,
less likely to
disappoint.
Forks you imagine
knocking at your door
late some night
tipsy and wanting
to sing all the old
songs.
      Knives,
you gave up
on knives ages ago.

Unfaithful

The scissors serious for a change
wonder what's with you.

You haven't played with them for weeks.
They miss the quick runs, the coupons.

They're sure you're cheating on them:
you've become a ripper,

one of those who folds and refolds the paper,
then scrapes a greasy thumbnail down

the edge. Then the slow, sacerdotal
tearing, as if the paper were precious, immortal,

not bits of blond space they could dice, one
edge tied behind their backs, in ten seconds, max.

The Way Things Work

Looking and looking and one day finding.
What's found doesn't matter. It's the
what you've been searching for, and that day
you find, you find more of it. Everywhere
you look, more, like in a dream, picking up
quarters stuck in river mud, the first quarter
leading to a second, which segues to another
and another, your pockets filling, you
can't stop, you're rich, everywhere
you look a shining, but you're not in a dream. This
is real. You keep finding the it but the more
you find the less and less you want until
before long you take all of what you've found
and just drop it, never once thinking that
by doing so you've laid a trap for the next person
looking for the very same thing. Never once
thinking you may have laid a trap for yourself.

De Kooning's Shirt

I want the shirt, the shirt
that screams jump, screams
fuck you and I want another
shot and who's the skirt.

I want the shirt, paint smears,
gobs of snot. Howl mommy,
spread your legs, here come
the jazz and bourbon fears.

Don't pasteurize my hurt.
Don't breathe my ten-foot smoke.
The rage phone's ringing, bub.
I want De Kooning's shirt.

Wrestling with the Angel

Why you hitting yourself?
Why you keep hitting yourself?
Stop hitting yourself.

Say uncle. If you say uncle, you won't have to keep hitting yourself.
Why you want to keep hitting yourself when all you have to say is uncle?
You know what your problem is: you lack faith, the power to believe,
    which is why you must keep hitting yourself.

If you don't stop hitting yourself, I'm going to have to tell someone.
I'm going to tell someone & then someone is going to hit you one.
You wouldn't like someone who's not you hitting you.
Someone not you doing the hitting may not stop.

Tell me, you like hitting yourself?
You like it because there's nobody else you can hit?
That's it, just keep hitting yourself.
Keep doing it & someone's going to come lock you up & throw away the
    key, & there'll be no someone there to save you from hitting yourself.

Right. You don't believe you're hitting yourself.
You think someone else is making you hit yourself.
So typical you can't assume responsibility for this hitting of yourself.
Well, there's no one here but you & me, & you would not want to
    accuse me of hitting you, right?
If I made you hit yourself, believe you me, you'd be crying for your
    mommy, & I don't see your mommy here.

Okay, you done, done hitting yourself?
Good, I'm glad you're done hitting yourself, this proud nation, even the
    angels in heaven, WE ARE GLAD.

I hope you feel better now you're done hitting yourself.

Let this be a lesson to you: you may hobble off, you may hide, but
    you will never escape the fact it is you and you alone who
    cannot stop hitting your own self.

There ought to be a law against people like you who can't stop hitting
    themselves.

Ten Spring Incidents

When you fear death go to the barber for a shave and a haircut.

Seen from far enough away you and those near you are not moving.

A question of metaphysics: when someone knocks on the bathroom door, then wiggles the handle, why do you close your eyes and say nothing?

You like to make things, she said. You heard this as, Things make to like you.

There are no unforgettable words.

What you need cannot be packed; what you do not need will always find you.

There are as many silences as there are people.

The sign read, "Nobody's business but your own."

You remember seeing a face at the window and knowing you shouldn't.

Gold

You want to buy gold, all you can,
which isn't much,

still you'd feel no better. Too much
wrong in the universe today.

Remember the last time
you were happy, really happy.

Lying on your belly before a window
overlooking the bay,

you could see smoke spiraling and twisting up
in the sky. Something big

burning. You didn't need sirens
to know help was coming.

When We Were Too Young to be Bad at Anything

they made us change into swimsuits we forgot in gym lockers until they
    smelled.

Made us wear white gym shorts with P.S. 18 stitched in gold, if we
    forgot our swimsuits.
If we forgot both, made us wear nothing, no matter what.

Made us swim the crawl, one at a time, two laps, there and back,
while Mr. Barris ragged on our weak strokes.

Made Kenny Powis, thalidomide baby, each finger like a tiny giblet tied
    to the bud of his arm,
made him swim so his fat-ass cheeks bobbled behind him like a
    parachute.

Made us laugh and laugh and laugh and laugh.

Bait

He sells it from an ice maker
by the side of the house on one of the town's
four dusty streets. Asks if I've used
live bait before but doesn't
wait for an answer. Darts his good
hand in the water and fishes
one out before I count *one Mississippi*.
Has a dog, a wolf he calls it,
one brown eye, one blue, keeps
nipping the cuffs of my jeans.
"He thinks you're a fawn," he says,
juggling the minnow in his hand
until the fin, I wonder if he was taught
it's the dorsal, peeks above his fingertips.
Holds up the other hand, the one
that looks as if it were ground and wrapped
in cellophane, says, "Imagine
this is your hook. You
need to slip it under the fin.
Too shallow, you lose your bait,
too deep, you hit spine, cripple
the fucker. And pike won't see it
if it ain't moving. You listening?"
Takes my tin bucket, fills it with water
I imagine as cold as the Arctic's
and a sawbuck's worth of writhing flesh.

Cured

Woman out walking,
pans in her hands.

Every next step
heavier

than the last. And the pans
in her hands:

imagine the grip, like a body hanging
from a cliff.

Those pans—fired
black, corrosive—the kind

dead fat
of animals is rubbed in.

Never to be washed, no meal ever
finished.

Ball

He threw a ball.
He threw a ball against the house.
He threw a ball every day.
In the morning. After lunch. At night. In the rain. In the snow.
Didn't matter.
He threw a ball and sometimes somebody watched.
But mostly they didn't:
he was just a boy throwing a ball.
It wasn't always the same ball
but it was a ball. And there was a house.
The house was always the same.
He threw a ball against a house with a number
on a street with a name.
It wasn't his ball or his house or his street because he knew
nothing was his.
He threw a ball.
He threw a ball knowing that there would be a day
he would no longer throw a ball.
This scared him, he might have said, if someone
had stopped to ask.
So he just threw a ball
and the ball always came back.

Tocsin

Some talk about a horse, a dead horse,
back up the road, by the cow pond,
and I go along, not to see the horse
exactly, but because there's this girl,
and it's Independence Day, also my birthday,
though I can't bring myself to tell anyone.
From a quarter mile off I say,
That's no horse, it's a cow, but someone,
this girl, says, It's a horse, and it is,
tipped on its side, legs stuck out stiff
like a knocked over chair. And there's still
this girl, so I get close to the horse,
and it's beautiful, the coat spit-shiny
in the sun, the flies glinting madly
like savage race cars as they swim over
the soft parts, asshole gaping, and I want,
no, I need to see this, and someone, maybe
the girl, says, What's his problem?
I hunker closer and I hear a voice,
maybe it's the weed, but I swear
it's a voice, telling, not words exactly,
and when it's done, I turn to everyone,
even the girl: I want them to see this shining
in my face, but they're gone, long gone.

Johnny Quest

Just a name I heard from my friend Michael,
the Michael who came to my apartment twenty years ago
to retrieve his Che and shake my hand like after a funeral
and promise he'd never write me, Michael of the snake-swallowing-its-tail
tattoo and rolling sailor's walk, as if he'd been born a merchant marine
instead of a fight choreographer and part-time bartender,
before that a dancer (he'd danced with Martha Graham!).
We were doing tequila shots and talking trash one night about
Melville and the *I Ching* and *Letters to a Young Poet*
when he leaned over to press a knuckle into my chest and tell me
he'd met this guy who called himself Johnny Quest, barely legal,
on a dance floor in Soho, and he could tell,
it was something he could feel plumb down to his balls—
and here he grabbed them, his not mine—Johnny was all possibility,
forget the made-up name, this Michael said.

True Genius

He couldn't,
but kept trying.
He practiced.
Bus. Study hall.
Bathroom.
Did and did and did
and never done.
All those years
and I see
he still can't
but now his can't is
what only he
can. Applaud
I tell these damned
hands. Applaud.

Rat

The morning they crucified him they made him wiggle
out of his jeans first, his hips shimmying a little dance
that might have been homoerotic if he hadn't been bleating
softly, tears slicking the corners of his juvenile mustache.
They realized then they'd forgotten to have him take off his shoes
so they made him squat in the mud and slick grass and unlace
his fresh white Converse, peel off his tube socks. After he obeyed
and stood up, one of them pointed to the moist streak on the back
of his underpants, and they all laughed, and this laughing saved him.
They intuitively understood, in the way of most torturers,
he could be no more naked than in his underpants, saggy,
bleached out and, though none of them would admit
to such knowledge and thus didn't use it as an opportunity for
further comedy, splotched with the scrim of virgin cum stains.
If you wonder why he didn't run or scream, it was simple: too many of them,
too few of him. Last to go, the T-shirt, revealing pink baby fat
and a nasty scar under his right nipple. "Breast removal,"
one of them barked. They let him keep his watch, burnished chrome
Timex, as if they wanted him to know the exact longitude of this,
his exquisite humiliation. They'd already taken off their own
belts, and then the biggest of them lifted his dead-feeling, boneless body
("Don't get any happy thoughts, faggot") while two others lashed
his upper arms to the chain-link. A fourth slapped his shaking legs
together to bind his ankles. They finished by simply walking away,
one of them startled out of a quasi-heavy metal funk long enough
to snap his belt once or twice, the way his brother had taught him,
and then slip it back on. They crucified the boy behind the bleachers
in back of the high school, beside the sumac, wild raspberries,
and weed clutter that served as a buffer between public and private,

where stoners drifted on silent paths to miss study hall, linear algebra,
    auto shop.
By now you must be thinking I know too much about what happened,
I was one of them, maybe even the boy himself, but this is no poem of
expiation. Even then, I lacked the courage of conscious cruelty. I simply
    imagine
this scene whispered behind open lockers for a week or two and then
    forgotten.
I too was a freshman that year, circa the Disco era, long enough ago
we compared our principal, with his mustache and Jewish haircut,
to Groucho Marx, the Groucho of "You Bet Your Life," when most
of the laughs had been shit-kicked out of him. Waiting to be picked last
for pick-up basketball or standing next to each other in a police line-up,
there wouldn't have been much to differentiate us, except I was shorter,
seemingly a more inviting target for the egg in the hair, the mouth
    gagged
with Barbasol. Yet, somehow, nobody ever asked me to come with them
to the fourth floor of a three-floor building. The summer before, I had
    begged
my father to send me to military school instead, but he didn't.
He said in life there was more to learn than learning. He was right.
Without knowing it, I was starting the long journey to the I you see
    before you,
the one who mastered the back alley mysteries, who learned
in the mad heat of panic what to take and what to leave behind.
Who taught himself the secret power of closing a door without
a soul hearing, stealing small change from the till, that the most powerful
    form
of invisibility doesn't come from magic, it's being seen, if peripheral,
always at the corner of others' eyes. Maybe, Nadiya, dearest, this is why,
though I handed you the book on rats on the long, boring drive to
    Annapolis,

knowing in doing so I would unlock your own unconscious desire to
    own such a pet,
your own first tentative step toward adulthood, I still did so.
If this poem isn't expiation or penance or forgiveness, what it is is what I
    want you
to see for the first time: me, your father, naked, stripped
to my underpants, here in this dark, stinking hole of my own making.
I am the rat of the title, camouflaged by the effluvia of words of a secret
    yet unavoidable life.

Burning Down Disneyland

Such a tiny house
here in the middle

of nowhere.
More of a phone booth

really, except
rather than a door

that folds in two, a regular
one, polished brass knob

and all. Almost Victorian, lovingly
crafted with the teensy

nails used in antique ship models.
Akimbo, as if dropped

from a star, a
machine unstapled

from time and place.
No floor even. As if whoever

set it here, set it
here for you alone

to cherish before
its imminent devastation.

Elegy

Did he dream of falling
and did he dream and never stop

falling in his dream
like a nickel dropped from a tall tall building

body revolving twisting and falling
but never touching bottom like in a dream

and when he fell
not in the dream but down those too real

steel-shanked stairs
did he remember the dream and if so

was his falling like the dream of his falling
the sound of his voice fallen

the one part never dreamt

Some Stories

Years later you realize some stories
you never write down. Some stories you only tell
and tell only to someone you'll never know well,
maybe after the loss of a sibling or an auto accident,
in a quiet place over a cigarette or coffee. Those
the stories you keep wedged so far down
in the pockets of your favorite jeans they become
the ash you brush from your daughter's dress
the night she goes on her first date. Those stories
you can forget for years and never forget a single detail,
their absence swelling inside you like an empty house.

To Guilt

I carry you like my wallet everywhere:
before I leave I feel to check you're still here.
Friend, you always are, you the currency
accepted in every one of my haunts and hideouts,
the credit card with no limits I pay off
inch by inch, never completely settling the tab.
Remember when we first met?
It must have been when I was a baby and I
could hear mother crying in the other room.
She knew you, too, better than I did of course, but hers
was different than mine: you. What I was doing
to make mother cry I don't know, except I know
you must. You always do. You've followed ever since,
synonymous shadow that can't stop limping
after me. I bought you suits, took you
to dances and dark alleys and drama classes, taught you
yourself in Russian in which you were already
fully fluent. Some mornings I wake and imagine
you're gone, caput, at last. O sweet luck!
A whole day daydreaming you've found someone else.
I don't mind you cheating, really, it's okay,
but by nightfall, I can't be without you
handing me something cool, rubbing the day's dumb
out of my shoulders, cooking this rice, fish, and wasabi,
blackened sesame seeds so good I could cry.

Aloneness

Turn the oven on and set it
as low as the gas can go.

Take the turkey pot pie
paid for
in the hush of the all-night service station,
your forearms still pink
and steaming
from washing other people's dishes,

and unwrap it gently, as a mother would,
so nothing can break.

Put the pie in the oven.

   Here's
the important part: do not
close
the oven door.

Flip on the game
                 or a radio.

Let the smell whisper slowly through
all the seams and creases.

When you're too famished to eat,
close the oven door.

Just Once

Come on, who wouldn't just once
like to be the bug-eyed alien with the badass ray gun?
How strange and wonderful
our world would seem
through purple-shuttered lenses. The bizarre sacks
of meat crumpling their soft faceplates,
leaking fuel.
How delicious to say,
I mean you no harm
and not mean a damned bit of it.
Hang in there. Help's coming, you'd riff
as you coolly flick the safety off
and flip the switch to FRAG
with the most beautiful tentacle in the universe.

The Good for Nothing and Left for Dead

Jalal-Abad, Kyrgyzstan

Even gunpowder mashed in their morning gruel
can't make dogs that hellfire mean,

as if ten millennia of roll over and play dead
could be steel-toed out of them.

Those lucky enough never to be mastered
unseen during daylight.

The bush trembling along the roadside,
the rusty growl below the floorboard, them.

Maroon yourself too long
before the same patch of faded wallpaper

and those are their eyes
razor-wired behind the fleur-de-lis.

Come night, as some unknown hand
banks the village lights street by street,

they haul their damned asses out
to raise their beautiful, busted snouts to the stars.

Love and joy and hope
a burnt stub in their mouths.

Their wild howls unslaked, like laughter.

Killing the Blue

Kant, Kyrgyzstan

Every morning my host bicycled to the airbase
and every night he returned with our dinner:

cucumbers, a few tomatoes, radishes still fragrant
of mud, a cabbage, somewhat weathered,

maybe last season's, and potatoes. He could fit three
in each hand, though his spanned no bigger than mine.

To peel potatoes like these, I learned touch,
a trigger sense of control. Not to peel

so much as to scrape skin off. My Leatherman
made him laugh; his knife was small, mostly

handle, and he let no one, not his wife,
the two girls or me, near it. When there'd still

been an air force, they'd stationed him
in East Germany and it was there, I guessed,

he got the tattoo. What was left—
the rays of a sun his youngest might draw,

but rather than eyes and a loopy smile
a scar, raised, like a fried egg.

When asked he smiled and motioned
to the other room where a Russian game show blared

on the TV, and then he took the shiv, for what else
can I call it, and mimed what his wife

had wanted and watched him do: vacate a rival's
name as easily as if it were the eye of a potato

or an enemy bullet. All summer he and I
watched the mountains to the south.

I hadn't heard an airplane in years.

Cleanly

Jalal-Abad, Kyrgyzstan

The women laughed when they saw my floor
and went to fill the bucket I'd bought
for bathing. They found old rags somewhere
and bent over so I could see the soft,
young spots behind their knees
and I had to turn my head, listening
to the slosh of water work its way
from one side of the room to the other.
By the time they finished, the apartment
was almost dry—a fine, late day dust
raised by cars and cooking fires and boys
pushing carts to market settling
over everything. They offered to come
the next day, and every day after, but I thanked
them, handed them an American paperback.
Winter flies buzzed between panes of glass,
the setting sun so bright I could only imagine
what lay beyond the pale pistachio hills.

City of the Infinite Lie

They're there, on every street corner,
particularly when you're not looking.

Cut, they do not bleed true.
To touch them in summer is to feel

a knot of heat;
in winter, a wet cheek freezes to them.

The billowing greatcoats suggest a mission.
The chiseled wonder of the retina.

They do not want
any more than they should.

Dreams of wings,
carapace shucked off,

of the missing tongues of bells,
the apocalyptic burrowing of worms.

Ever throw your arm around a shadow?
Ever hit your head with a hammer?

They're there. Acetylene
consonants, illegible footprints.

Bucket tumbling down a poisoned well.

Blackout Drinking

The one called
Bill shows up nights
and slides a crisp Jackson
under his coaster,
the cool heft
of the first draft as familiar
and unexpected
as the doorknob of a house
whose phone number
he's long since misplaced,
each sip, uncounted,
slurrying the figures around him,
the shiny music and gabble
disintegrating into the anonymity
of gravel under car tires,
the lights winking off
one by one
the farther he drinks himself
until there are only
the smudges of trees whisking by
and the darkness, half-remembered,
that lies between them.

Things Not Done in the Past Five Years

I did not lend a single howler monkey a single power tool no matter the howling.

I did not enter into any secret treaties of warm and eternal friendship.

I did not rearrange the Bill of Rights to the syncopated beat of my belief.

I did not levitate in the back of a stolen truck, share a Popsicle with Siamese twins, or meditate on the hairlines of those who would hurt me.

I have refused, on principle, to pray to any subterranean gods.

Or to tickle the gravid chins of cue balls.

I did not scratch an unmentionable body part and imagine I was as famous as Toulouse-Lautrec.

If I lusted in my heart, it was never for anything I wouldn't admit to Christopher Smart's cat.

I never took a potshot, with malice aforethought, with a pump action .22, at Air Force One.

I did not finish a short history of beggars or reinvent zero.

I did not wake, shouting to nobody in particular, Everyone is a version, sometimes corrupt, of everyone else.

I may have gotten down on my hands and knees on the new spring grass but did not do so to recall the lost smell of anyone I've known.

I didn't dare dream.

Or do my taxes.

Or trim the dog's nails.

Or tip a single pretty hotel maid anywhere.

I did not think how there will be no more sun billions of years from now.

Or of all my great grandchildren's stories and how I will never be a character, even salacious, in one of them.

Or if I fell from a bridge would I as I was falling ask for the last dozen or so seconds back.

If I tried on many hats, none was impossible.

I did not stand in the desert silence and follow the flight of a hummingbird and fear for the petrified gears of its heart.

I never opened the back door of my house to let in the usual ghosts.

(In the past five years I admit I have done much but little that might trouble the sleep of a dying saint.)

If I climbed a mountain then sent you a cheap rhinestone postcard, I did not do so because it was there but because I wasn't.

I have not cried for the sun.

Packs

We were running in a field on a track
if one could call an elliptical rut gutted
with rock and bits of bone that

and we must have been talking
about our bowels or a neighbor
stealing electricity our bodies making
the good clean sound running bodies make
so if we saw the kids we didn't really
until they formed a pack
some ran parallel to us not close
as if they were tracking sleek new beasts in jeeps
and they started a singsong taunt
and one loosened his pants to
moon us hairless balls jiggling we laughed

which is when they started throwing
whatever they got their small hands on
in our general direction and we kept running
if we willed it it could not happen

who knows how it might've ended
if one hadn't picked up a bigger rock and thrown it
almost hitting you you were a woman
god dammit that's when I went a little nuts
you remember how they all froze
like in a backyard game of Simon Says
as the rock slashed through them I can hear it

if it'd gone a few inches left or right it would've
brained an unlucky one maybe
killed because I'd grown up
in the U.S.A. where every boy
by five years is given a hardball and a mitt
and the time and the place to learn
how not to throw like a sissy

the rock the same thrown at you
I can feel how heavy it was
how strong I could be as it left my hand

Voodoo

Apologize
         now. Before it's too late.

Practice, finally,
         the small habits of penance.

What I volunteered of you:
         eyes, nose, knees, baby toe, thirty-three

vertebrae, your
         extraordinary meridians, the places my lips

kissed, like Xs
         on a treasure map.

Tools? Anything
         rat-tooth rabid: bobby pin, swizzle stick, potato

peeler, splinter
         from a park bench, nail. See:

what pierces
         pulses, quivers,

as if it were the thing
         pierced. Because this thing

is you, is
         what you made me

make you.

Yes,

they are good,
        but their house has no door.

They are wise,
        yet their ladder has no step.

Though kind,
        their cup has no lip.

They are strong,
        but their stone does not bloom.

Just,
        yet their sky lost its name.

If happy,
        their dog has no tail.

Afterwards

With so much to talk about, it's amazing
we can still manufacture silence.

But this is what we are left with
as you brace your back against the kitchen sink

letting the water run and run.

Imagine Adam, afterwards.

Trying to make sense of this gap in his side.
Holding his hands out to Eve, cupped,

as if trying to catch the coming rain.

How You Will Remember Me When I'm Dead and Buried

I don't mind anymore what you do to me.
Go ahead. Zipper me with scars, loads of them.

Five o'clock shadow, a mullet, Spock ears,
goatee, ice cream cone breasts and tiny pegs

in the neck, like Frankenstein's monster.
Thirty-two teeth, who needs them?

If you have a crayon, an orange schnozz
some ankle-biter might try to reach for and honk.

I hope you get into the spirit of the thing,
sketching in wings, zits, Rolling Stone lips,

and dead center a giant L, Magic-Markered.
But when you're done, one last request:

the honor of a mustache, waxed like
Dali's, the one I never will grow,

no matter how long the wisp of forked tail
(nice touch) wags behind these twin blacked eyes.

I Won't Need Billy Collins Anymore

Someday I know something'll strike me
and I'll get up and saunter down the hallway

to the office of my boss who doesn't look
at all like Billy Collins, except for her eyes,

mild as the blue lines on this pad of legal bond
that keep me from spilling off the edge

and never finding my way back.
I'll ask her to a café where we'll sip tea.

I'll pretend the cars sliding by don't sound
like the ocean eternally punishing the beach

for being a beach, and I'll tip my chair back
and tell her about what it's like swimming

halfway across a timber lake at twilight
before the wind's gotten up, or how leaving

will be like slipping out a side door with
a pair of snowshoes slung over my shoulders,

though it hasn't snowed in these parts for years.

Losing the Nouns

First the names go,
then
the nouns.

What goes last will make
no difference.

Practice dying.

The Stars Are Too Far to Need Faces

I am writing this poem to you on Monday.
I will bring it to the post office and mail it.
And then a truck will come pick it up
and bring it to a different truck and this
truck will deliver it to the post office where
you live, and then a postman will drive it
to your mailbox and you will find
this poem, and it will be Wednesday
or Thursday. Which will mean it will be
only a few more days before I see you
again because I will fly on Saturday while
you are in your art class. Maybe while
you're in your art class you can think of
me, and you can draw an airplane and
in one of the windows you can crayon me,
and I will be waving at you and smiling.
Make the day sunny, with just a cloud
or two, and if there are any birds, make sure
they're small birds and not too hungry.

The Old Game

The children in the park I am watching
but not watching are playing an old game,

what my generation called cops and robbers,
my father's cowboys and Indians,

but I cannot see what prop
they hold in their empty hands

as they layer death all around them, each heart
break more propulsive than the last,

until there's only one left standing,
the winner, lone survivor, a he or a she,

I can't tell from this distance,
nor maybe do I want to, who looks around

at the emptiness for some dizzying time
before taking whatever invisibility

he or she holds and turns it
against itself. I imagine a wry, self-conscious smile

before the deed and perhaps the fleeting thought
the problem isn't so much with ourselves

but with the world, before she or he falls alone
no longer.

And then a stillness broken only by laughter
and the children I am watching but not watching

get up, brush the cut grass
from their bellies and knees, and start again.

ABOUT THE POET

Kurt Olsson's first collection of poetry, *What Kills What Kills Us*, won the Gerald Cable Book Award and was published by Silverfish Review Press in 2007. In 2008, the book was awarded the Towson University Prize for Literature, given annually to the best book published the previous year by a Maryland writer, as well as named Best Poetry Book of 2008 by Peace Corps Writers.

Olsson's poems have appeared in many journals, including the *Alaska Quarterly Review*, *Antioch Review*, *FIELD*, *Gettysburg Review*, *The New Republic*, *Poetry*, *Southern Review*, and *The Threepenny Review*. He also has two chapbooks to his credit: *I Know Your Heart, Hieronymus Bosch* and *Autobiography of My Hand*.